My Purrfect Friend

Designed By Roni Akmon

Compiled By Nancy Akmon

Written By Karen Choppa

Illustrations by Gre`Gereardi

Blushing Rose Publishing

San Anselmo, California

For:
Karen

From:
Patty

Date:
Christmas 2005

Cover Illustration and interior illustrations by Gre` Gerardi. These illustrations are reprinted
with the permission of the Balliol Corporation. Text written by Karen Choppa.
Designed by Roni Akmon
Compiled by Nancy Akmon

ISBN# 1-884807-60-7

Blushing Rose Publishing
P.O. Box 2238
San Anselmo, Ca. 94979
www.blushingrose.com

Printed in China

WE HAVE SUCH FUN TOGETHER!

BEING WITH YOU IS LIKE A WALK IN THE GARDEN

YOU ALWAYS KNOW WHEN I NEED A HUG

When I blow out my birthday candles,
I'd wish for you all over again

You dance to your own music

SOMETIMES YOU'RE A MYSTERY...

...SOMETIMES YOU'RE A CLOWN

YOU ALWAYS PLAY FAIR

MISCHIEF IS OUR MIDDLE NAME

YOU KNOW WHEN I NEED MOTHERING...

...AND YOU KNOW WHEN I NEED TO BE LEFT ALONE

You let me cry on your shoulder

gré gerardi ©

YOU KNOW HOW TO MAKE ME SMILE

You're really an angel in disguise

You're table manners may need some work...

...BUT YOU'RE THE BEST GROOMED

You're always ready for "Let's Pretend"

You let me join in your adventures

You can be shy...

...BUT SOMETIMES YOU LIKE TO BE THE CENTER OF ATTENTION

You're always on my side

YOU LIKE TO "HORSE AROUND"

EVERYONE'S ALWAYS HAPPY TO SEE YOU

YOU LIKE TO RUN BAREFOOT
THROUGH THE GRASS, TOO

MENU
Salmon Soufflé
Mouse Mousse
Rodent Ragout
Tuna TREATS
Sardines on
CRACKERS
Hot "ROVERS" on
Rolls

Catnip Cookie
Sweet Cream
LIVER LAYERCAKE

EVERY DAY'S A PICNIC WITH YOU

You find us the best places to share...

...AND NEW THINGS TO TRY

YOU MAKE HOLIDAYS AND SPECIAL OCCASIONS EVEN BRIGHTER

YOU'RE BEAUTIFUL THROUGH AND THROUGH

YOU'RE A KID AT HEART JUST LIKE ME

YOU CAN EVEN MAKE BATHTIME FUN

You can even make doing chores fun

WITH YOU BY MY SIDE, I CAN FACE ANYTHING

AND WHEN THE DAY IS OVER, I KNOW YOU'LL BE THER

OMORROW